T0142201

WORDS *of* INSPIRATION

Darrel Everhart

WESTBOW
P R E S S®
A DIVISION OF THOMAS NELSON
& ZONDERVAN

WestBow Press books may be ordered through
booksellers or by contacting:

WestBow Press
A Division of Thomas Nelson & Zondervan
1663 Liberty Drive
Bloomington, IN 47403
www.westbowpress.com
1 (866) 928-1240

ISBN: 978-1-5127-8407-7 (sc)
ISBN: 978-1-5127-8406-0 (e)

Library of Congress Control Number: 2017906229

Print information available on the last page.

WestBow Press rev. date: 04/24/2017

NEW DIRECTION

I have traveled down life's path,
Heading into the great unknown,
Facing obstacle after obstacle,
Praying to God my path to be shown,

Suffering with anxiety and depression,
But still traveling on,
Wondering if I would ever be happy,
Hoping my depression would be gone.

I started having negative thoughts,
Telling me I had done something wrong,
Telling me that it was all my fault,
That I had suffered so long.

I had almost given up on happiness,
Thinking there wasn't anything I could do,
Just when things got their darkest,
My God's grace came shining through.

He brought someone special into my life,
Who gave me hope for a better day.
She caused me to hear the right things,
And showed me the right way.

God had never forgotten about me,
He was there every mile.
When I called on Him and believed,
He helped me regain my smile.

I no longer had to deal with depression,
I had finally passed the test.
Now I know that no matter what,
I can overcome the rest.

I now have a new lease on life,
I see new opportunities everywhere.
I know I will come out victorious,
Because God is always there.

GUIDANCE

In our lives we sometimes have doubts,
Times when we're not quite sure.
We can easily push doubts aside,
As long as our hearts are pure.

As long as you believe in God,
And have faith the size of a mustard seed,
You'll never have to experience lack,
For He provides us with all we need.

It's true that we will face obstacles daily,
Things will definitely get in the way.
It doesn't prevent us from reaching our destiny,
As long as we ask God for guidance everyday.

No one ever said life would be easy,
But God always has a plan.
You may not see what's ahead,
But always know that He can.

Our lives are like a book,
That was written long ago.
This book can end in victory,
As long as faith you're willing to show.

There's no need for us to get discouraged,
God has us in the palm of His hand.
Just trust in Him to guide you,
And you'll end up in the promised land.

FREE WILL

Free will is an amazing concept.
It comes from God above.
Giving us the choice to hate,
As well as the option to love.

We have the option to believe,
Or we can choose to doubt.
He will never make us do anything,
Because that's not what free will is about.

We all have many choices to make,
Which will ultimately decide our fate.
Even though we sometimes make poor choices,
Be encouraged that it's never too late.

God already knows what choice we'll make,
Whether it will be good or bad.
He has already planned for this choice,
So there's no need to be sad.

We don't ever have to be discouraged,
Over the choices we will face.
God has placed all the right options,
To get us to the right place.

We should always look to God for guidance,
So we will be where we need to be.
He said all things will work for our benefit,
Trust God and you will see.

DAILY WALK

Every day when we arise,
And begin a brand new day,
We go through our morning rituals,
Before we go on our way.

Before we do anything else,
We should never forget to pray,
So we can find out exactly,
What God wants us to do today.

Every day is a new day,
With new challenges to face,
By going to Him for guidance,
We can be lead to the right place.

All through the day we need Him,
To tell us what we are to do,
So when we come across obstacles,
God can lead us through.

And when our travels are finished,
And we have nowhere else to go.
We should go to Him with praise,
For our gratitude we should show.

Just going to worship on Sunday,
Isn't what being a Christian is all about.
It's about a daily walk with Jesus,
So from His book you won't be left out.

NEW DAY

Sometimes it's really hard,
To forget the mistakes of the past,
To get over the shame,
It doesn't have to last.

Every time we call on God,
And ask for forgiveness of our sin.
If we will repent He will forgive us,
And never remember it again.

Every day is truly a new day,
We should have a new outlook on life.
We don't have to carry the shame,
And deal with all the strife.

Leave the past behind you,
And look to the future ahead.
You will find new blessings before you.
Forget all your dread.

Constantly ask for guidance,
He has new blessings in store.
He will fulfill your wishes,
And give you so much more.

He is a forgiving God.
He will give you what you need.
You are a child of the most high God.
He wants you to succeed.

PERFECTION

As you may have already realized,
No one has reached perfection.
We all have weaknesses in life,
That can be corrected through daily direction.

We may never reach true perfection,
But we must constantly strive.
Through faith, prayer and effort,
We are promised that we will thrive.

God has never expected us to be perfect,
He just expects us to live a godly life.
By calling on Him every day,
We can overcome all the strife.

We must always focus on positivity,
And leave all negativity behind.
Then we have the possibility,
Of a more perfect life to find.

If we keep looking to Him for guidance,
There's no obstacle we can't overcome.
No one is exempt from His assistance,
It doesn't matter where you're from.

Although we may never be perfect,
To not try we can't afford.
You'll always have a chance at heaven,
As long as you keep Him as your Lord.

MINOR IRRITANTS

As we go through our daily routine,
We'll suffer with an occasional irritation.
God uses these minor issues,
To mold His awesome creation.

Just like a potter does,
When he's working with clay.
He has to mold it daily,
God does us the same way.

Just like a wood craftsman,
When he's working with wood.
He has to sand the rough edges,
So his creation will come out good.

We are always being molded,
To make us into what we're to be.
Stay strong through this process,
So a more perfect creation we may see.

God always knows what He's doing,
He uses these issues for our good.
He just wants us to be able,
As only He knows we should.

Have faith and stay strong,
And you will make it through.
God can see the final product,
A more perfect you.

FRESH START

Every day that we arise,
We can consider a fresh start,
As long as we look to God for guidance,
And keep Him in our heart.

In spite of mistakes we have made,
We can proceed with a clean slate.
God is willing to forgive and forget,
And guide us towards our fate.

Everyone can experience victory,
We just have to trust God to lead the way.
We must have faith in His methods,
And be very careful in what we say.

When we make Him our Lord and Savior,
And allow Him into our heart.
We are guaranteed forgiveness,
So that we can make a fresh start.

We still may face trials and tribulations,
To make us better Christians than we were,
But never lose sight of our ultimate goal,
Because with God's guidance we can be sure.

As long as we praise Him daily,
His love and mercy will never be gone,
Because no matter what happens,
God is always on the throne.

FORGIVENESS

Sometimes no matter what we do,
Or how we treat our fellow man.
Others may do things we may not like,
And treat us any way they can.

We don't have to like what was done,
Or being called out of our name.
We can't react to the incident,
Or treat them exactly the same.

As Christians we are taught to forgive,
And just turn the other cheek.
We have to overlook the offense,
And just appear as if we are meek.

If we are ever to be forgiven,
We have to do the same.
Never seeking to gain revenge,
Or handing out blame.

God is willing to forgive any trespass,
And we should be able to do the same thing.
We are never above forgiving someone,
Remember God is our king.

So we must always remember to forgive,
No matter what others do.
Our forgiveness is a stake,
And starting over anew.

A SOLEMN PRAYER

I thank You Jesus,
For all You do,
For giving me hope,
That I'll make it though.

No matter what I face,
From day to day,
I know I'll survive,
By doing things Your way.

I require Your guidance,
In my everyday walk.
I always speak positively,
Whenever I talk.

I know You have a plan,
No matter what the situation.
I just have to have faith,
That You're never on vacation.

I know You have me,
In the palm of Your hand.
You are on the throne,
And You rule the land.

I give You all the glory,
For every single thing.
And want You to know,
You're forever my king.

BEACON OF HOPE

These words that I write,
Come from God above.
In hope of inspiring,
Those who know God's love.

I consider myself fortunate,
To possess this gift.
My only wish for God's children,
Is your spirit to lift.

Like a lighthouse on the coast,
Gives hope to sailors at sea.
My goal with these words,
Is help someone be all they can be.

I'm not perfect by far,
In every single way.
But I look to Him for guidance,
Every single day.

Sometimes we experience setbacks,
And make mistakes along the way.
I hope these words inspire you,
To get on your knees and pray.

We all need inspiration daily,
And that's what I set out to do.
So in tough times you won't forget,
God will see you through.

AWESOME BEAUTY

Have you ever taken a good look,
At all the scenery around.
It doesn't matter where you look,
There is beauty to be found.

If you drive through the mountains,
And gaze at the foliage in fall.
There's a diverse mixture of colors,
And God created it all.

Or you could walk along the beach,
And marvel at the sunset.
You will be amazed at the sight,
It's as inspiring as it can get.

And through the countryside at spring,
And all the flowers in full bloom.
A more awesome sight to behold,
Like a blushing bride to her groom.

We as God's people possess this beauty,
Like all the birds in the air.
You don't have to look very hard,
God's awesome beauty is everywhere.

So next time you venture out,
In the up and coming days.
Gaze at the beauty around you,
And remember to God goes all the praise.

DOUBTS

As we continue our daily walk,
With Jesus by our side.
We still face obstacles,
Trying to break our stride.

As people we sometimes have doubts,
That surface within our mind.
We often come up with questions,
With answers we need to find.

It's alright to call on God,
And be honest about our doubt.
He realizes that we aren't perfect,
Being honest is what it's all about.

We never need to conceal,
The imperfections that we possess,
God won't turn His back on us,
And let us deal with all the stress.

Our doubts will often draw God in,
To prove to us that He's there.
He can see the faith in our hearts,
So our doubts we can freely share.

Just remember we are not perfect,
God doesn't expect us to be.
Always be truthful with Him,
And His glory you will see.

MEDIOCRITY

Are you one of those people,
Who are content with where you are.
You are satisfied with your life,
You're not praying that God will raise the bar.

It's alright to be happy,
But God's ready to give you more.
You don't have to settle for mediocrity,
He doesn't expect us to be poor.

Your Father has plans for you,
He wants His children to succeed.
There's no limit to how far you can go,
For God will supply your every need.

Keep praying and have faith,
And doing what He tells you to do.
Your cup will truly run over,
He has awesome blessings in store for you.

Right now He's lining things up,
Just get ready to receive the excess.
You won't receive it till your ready,
His faithful children He loves to bless.

Whenever you go to Him in prayer,
Keep your hearts dreams in mind.
Don't just pray to barely get by,
And His overwhelming blessings you'll find.

DIVISION

The world is in turmoil,
Riots and protests everywhere.
Division amongst the masses,
Everyone is filled with despair.

There's uncertainty all over,
No direction to be found.
Destruction in the cities,
Confusion is abound.

There's no peace in the world,
Satan's influence is alive.
Desperation is a motivator,
Mob rule seems to thrive.

Even with all this going on,
God is still on the throne.
No matter how it appears,
Hope is still not gone.

Unity is still a possibility,
People are in need of direction.
All of this confusion created,
By something as simple as an election.

Everyone should take a moment,
And seek answers from God above.
All these problems can be solved,
With a lot of faith and love.

We could stop the devil's rampage,
And get everything straight.
With the help of God in heaven,
America can once again be great.

IN SICKNESS AND IN HEALTH

We all experience those mornings,
When we don't feel quite right.
When it feels like just getting up,
Would require an uneasy fight.

We know we have things to do,
Or places we need to go,
But our bodies aren't cooperating,
Causing us to move real slow.

Laying in bed seems a better choice,
Although we'll not get anything done.
If we just force ourselves to rise,
Half the battle will be won.

Just tell yourself that you're able,
There are things that you must do.
And just lean on God's arm,
And He will surely get you through.

Don't let your mind hold you back,
Let your faith help you rise.
You don't want to miss a good day,
Or miss out on God's prize.

Never let yourself be held back,
From what God has in store.
His blessings are worth rising up,
And He promises even more.

PROMISES

No matter how you live your life,
You will have problems appear.
Sometimes through our weaknesses,
Sometimes because of things we hear.

These problems sometimes confuse us,
They seem to get in our way.
You may think that they are too big,
But they could disappear today.

You may not see an end to them,
Just remember that God always has a plan.
No matter how long you've had them,
The problem may seem big, but God's greater than.

Through faith you can always overcome,
Everything will truly come to pass.
Continue praying and have faith,
The Lord will not allow it last.

He uses these problems to show,
His blessings in an awesome way.
He wants to show that it had to be God,
And there's nothing anyone can say.

When you encounter obstacles in life,
Know that the end has been set.
You are in store for God's favor,
You're as blessed as you can get.

HELPING OTHERS

Ever since I was younger,
I've been willing to do what I could.
Someone has always needed me,
Which made me feel good.

Helping others who are in need,
Is something I like to do.
We all need help at times,

A fact I find to be true.

I know the Lord would expect us,
To do whatever we can.
We should always be willing,
To help our fellow man.

Back in the days people traded services,
Because we all have a special skill.
Although things have changed over time,
Some things never will.

We are all basically brethren,
Part of one big family.
Taking time to help one another,
Is what God likes to see.

It doesn't take very much effort,
To help a friend in need.
God looks favorably upon us,
Whenever we do a good deed.

SATAN

Satan is quite active today,
Causing confusion among the masses.
Pitting one side against the other,
To see this you don't need glasses.

In believing that God exists,
Then Satan does too.
There's no need to fear him,
He can only do what you let him do.

God will always be stronger,
And with God you'll always win.
Satan only has control,
When you're living in sin.

Never let Satan deceive you,
And know that he will try.
He already knows that he can't win,
And we surely know why.

God created the whole world,
And everything that you can see.
As long as you live for Him,
You will experience victory.

Denounce Satan in Jesus' name,
And he will have to go away.
Only God will be present,
When you face your judgment day.

MY GOD

We have been taught through the years,
By others what God has said.
The Bible has been used like a textbook,
We have constantly heard it read.

Everyone out there has a different interpretation,
Of all the teachings contained within.
It has a detailed history of the world,
From the very time it was said to begin.

Scientists and scholars have disputed it,
Claiming the teachings within are not true.
But all through the ages evidence has been found,
So believing or not is totally up to you.

I'm often confused at the ideology,
Used by people to prove that God isn't real.
When so many biblical events are proven to be true,
I myself am not confused on how to feel.

Through my life I have done the research,
And I have no doubt that God is alive.
Without God's favor, love and blessings,
The world couldn't possibly continue to thrive.

It's up to each individual to make a decision,
As to whether they use the Bible as a handbook.
As for my family there is no question,
For guidance to God we will always look.

SMILE

There are times when things go wrong,
When things don't seem to go right.
Everyday no matter what you do,
Everything feels like a fight.

Everyone experiences days like these,
But we can't let them drag us down.
God is still working on our behalf,
He still wears the crown.

He knows what is going on all the time,
His favor is constantly on our life.
Show faith and smile through it all,
And you can overcome all the strife.

To reach the destiny we have in store,
We have to allow God to lead the way.
No matter what obstacle you face,
Just remember at God's feet let it lay.

He knows what is coming your way,
He already has a plan.
We shouldn't worry about anything,
But doing what we can.

Constantly go to God for guidance,
For only He knows the way.
Soon we should experience peace,
And be able to enjoy every day.

SOWING

During the planting season,
All farmers sow their seeds.
The seeds they choose to sow,
Are based on their needs.

They realize that what they sow,
Is what will eventually grow.
They don't have to guess,
Through experience they know.

As Christians we sow seeds as well,
We accomplish this a different way.
We go around sowing seeds,
By our actions and what we say.

We can share the same assurance,
As long as we sow seeds that are good.
Sow seeds of positivity and happiness,
Just the same as Jesus would.

We will reap whatever we sow,
We ultimately possess the choice.
Unlike the farmers everywhere,
We sow using our voice.

Always keep a positive attitude,
And do whatever God tells you to do.
You'll receive blessings for what you've sown,
For God's promises always come true.

MORALS

What is happening in the world today,
Our moral values are going downhill.
There are people all over the world,
Who give a whole new meaning to free will.

Has our government become so corrupt,
That literally anything goes.
What will be legal in the near future,
We are at a point where who knows.

We really need to be careful people,
Doesn't everyone know that God can see.
He still has control of the world,
And from His wrath you cannot flee.

It's time that we take control,
And put a stop to all that is wrong.
We don't have to allow these atrocities,
Because God won't for very long.

Have we forgotten about Sodom and Gomorrah,
For we're heading in the same direction.
We all need to get on our knees,
It's about time for a little reflection.

God can be very forgiving,
But we can't wait until it's too late.
If we don't do something soon,
We could be doomed to the same fate.

PEOPLE

We live in a diverse society,
Different kinds of people everywhere.
The differences aren't always apparent,
But they are most assuredly there.

We shouldn't spend our time,
Paying attention to what's on the outside.
Looks aren't important to God,
When He decides in whose heart to reside.

We should always treat our fellow man,
They way we wish to be treated.
When we choose to do this,
All prejudice can be defeated.

Even if someone chooses to be mean,
And to always treat you unfair.
Continue to show respect for them,
And take it to God in prayer.

We don't have to treat others wrong,
Because of how they choose to be.
We are not responsible for their behavior,
Only God can make them see.

We must learn to embrace diversity,
For we are not all the same.
We must always love our neighbors,
And pray for them in Jesus' name.

CHANGE YOUR FOCUS

Lately have you found yourself,
Worrying about what's going on in your life.
Constantly praying to God,
To remove or ease your strife.

Take a step back and look around,
At all the others in your life you meet.
Do you really think for a minute,
That you're the only one living with defeat.

Are your problems really larger,
Are you really suffering more.
There are people with bigger problems,
In this you can be sure.

Try helping someone else with their issues,
And stop focusing on your own.
Soon you will have a better prospective,
When compassion for others you have shown.

We should always be mindful of others,
And help out whenever we can.
Our problems may pale in comparison,
To those of our fellow man.

If we stop always thinking of ourselves,
And start helping others with what they face.
God will take care of our needs,
And the world will become a better place.

STUDY

Have you ever taken the time,
Or even given it a thought,
To actually know about God's promises,
Could prevent you from becoming distraught.

To become familiar with His word,
Requires one to do more than read.
The Bible isn't just a book,
It's our life manual indeed.

It explains how it all began,
How we got to where we are.
God created the world with words,
Right down to the smallest star.

It tells of God's great sacrifice,
Because He loves us so much.
He has brought the dead back to life,
With only His awesome touch.

The Bible is full of stories and lessons,
To teach us how to live each day.
With a strong commitment to study,
We learn how to live His way.

As children of the most high God,
He knows that we can succeed.
With our Lord and the Holy Bible,
We truly have all we need.

MIRACLES

Have you ever said I need a miracle,
Even though you didn't believe.
You couldn't see it happening,
You didn't think you would receive.

Don't get stuck thinking small,
Because our God is great.
Just remember that all you see,
Our God did create.

Nothing is impossible with God,
There isn't anything that He can't do.
God has control of everything,
No matter what He will get you thru.

Have faith in God on everything,
And know that God is there.
He is by your side no matter what,
As well as no matter where.

God has performed miracles before,
When no one else could see a way.
So it stands to reason,
That He still does today.

Walking in faith has its' benefits,
If it can be done God can.
There's no obstacle too big,
It's all a part of God's plan.

CHILDREN

Anytime you have questions,
Regarding the future of mankind.
Just look at the children around you,
In them will be answers to find.

Children are often reflections,
Of their own environment.
Mimicking all they have seen,
Everything should be apparent.

What they are taught early,
Will aide them later on.
Good or bad it sticks with them,
Even when they are grown.

Moral values can't always be taught,
Some is based on what they see.
How they see others act daily,
They're also watching you and me.

Are we setting the right examples,
Showing our children the right way.
Always remembering God's teachings,
And living it every single day.

Do we treat our neighbors as family,
Walking around with a smile on our face.
Teach the children while they are young,
And our future will be a brighter place.

TIME

Time is a precious commodity,
It's something you cannot buy.
You only have what you have,
No matter how hard you try.

None of us really know how much,
Time any of us possess.
And when it seems to run short,
It tends to cause us stress.

Just make sure that you utilize,
Each second like it were your last.
And don't forget to take time for God,
Because it goes by fast.

Don't get stressed over time,
Enjoy every last minute.
Be happy that God created the world,
And was glad to put us in it.

Time is quite precious,
But it's more important how it's spent.
We all have a purpose in life,
That's why we were sent.

God has given us enough time,
To do what we must do.
He promises us eternal life,
Whenever our task is through.

EASY WAY

When your life seems a little off,
Things don't feel quite right.
You can call upon the Lord,
It doesn't have to be night.

When you're waiting on a blessing,
That hasn't shown up yet.
Have no fear and don't worry,
God has everything all set.

Always have faith in everything,
God is always there.
And He treats us all,
With tender loving care.

Don't let any situation confuse you,
God already has a plan.
He is always in control,
We're always in the palm of His hand.

Keep focusing on doing what is right,
So you don't have to fear.
No matter what you face,
God is always near.

Life can be so simple,
We are destined to succeed.
We can relax in the knowledge,
That we have all we need.

OVER THE TOP

When you kneel to pray at night,
Do you pray to just barely get by.
Are you fully content in your situation,
That you don't reach for the sky.

God is constantly working on us,
Making us better with each passing day.
Helping us to reach our full potential,
Which can only be achieved His way.

Don't get passive in your prayers,
Remember you have to ask to receive.
He has promised us so much,
And you know God doesn't deceive.

Look back at where you were,
And compare that to where you are.
If you've allowed God to mold you,
He has definitely raised the bar.

Don't allow yourself to become complacent,
You may not have that far to go.
His work on you may be about finished,
You just never know.

Pray for an abundance in everything,
Remember God supplies your every need.
Remain humble in your everyday life,
And you can't help but succeed.

THE MIRROR

Every time you look in the mirror,
What is it that you see.
Are you content where you are,
Are you who you thought you would be.

Are you doing what you're supposed to do,
Living like you know you should.
Following the guidance of the Lord,
Always treating everyone good.

Do you help others when you can,
Showing respect for the elderly.
Don't become discouraged,
If this isn't what you see.

Think back to who you were,
And realize that you've came a long way.
The Lord is changing and molding you,
Telling you what to do and what to say.

Remember you are a work in progress,
He has you in the palm of His hand.
He has everything under control,
He rules throughout the land.

Take another good hard look,
And be happy with what you see.
Continue to give God the glory,
For what you'll eventually be.

WAIT

We all have struggles in life,
Issues that we have to face.
Times when things get hard,
And it feels like we are in a bad place.

It consumes your every thought,
And true focus is hard to achieve.
Causing us to question ourselves,
Not knowing what to believe.

This is where our faith in God is tested,
To see if we can pass the test.
We have to wait on the Lord,
For only He knows what's best.

Just because a solution hasn't appeared yet,
Doesn't mean it's not on the way.

It's easy for us to get discouraged,
Just be careful what you say.

He does things in His own time,
But He is never late.
Just wait patiently on Him,
And you'll receive your fate.

Everything has already been decided,
It was decided long ago.
Just wait on things to work out,
And always allow your faith to show.

BAD TIMES

Do you find yourself dwelling,
On all the bad things going on.
Forgetting all the good things,
Until your peace is gone.

It's easier for us to remember,
All the bad times we've had.
Not thinking about our blessings,
When we are actually glad.

Think for a moment about God's blessings,
And how special they made you feel.
Bad times are meant to be forgotten,
So happiness can be found for real.

You don't have to hold on to bad memories,
But to the good ones hold fast.
Good memories will always produce,
A smile that will last.

Next time you kneel to pray,
Thank God for all He's done for you.
Instead of having a long list,
Of things you need Him to do.

God is good all the time,
Bad times come and go.
Always be thankful for your blessings,
And don't forget to let Him know.

CHRISTMAS

It's time for family and friends,
To come together to celebrate.
The most wonderful gift ever received,
That would ultimately seal our fate.

God made the ultimate sacrifice,
And gave us His only Son.
He did that because He loves us dearly,
With this gift a new era begun.

He knew how we would react,
But He did it anyway.
This gift from long ago,
Still benefits us today.

At this time be very thankful,
Nothing you receive could ever compare.
His gift was given to all,
It shows that there's nothing He won't share.

Instead of thinking of ourselves,
And what we'll get this year.
Take time to give God the glory and praise,
Just because you are here.

Enjoy a very merry Christmas,
With all those you hold dear.
And thank God for His blessings,
And pray for peace in the coming year.

Printed in the United States
By Bookmasters